Instructor's Manual | Clinical Social Work: Knowledge and Skills

Instructor's Manual For

Clinical Social Work | Knowledge and Skills

Helen Northen and Marie Weil

Second Edition

New York | Columbia University Press

Columbia University Press
New York Chichester, West Sussek

Casebound editions of Columbia University Press books are printed on permanent and durable acid-free paper.

Printed in the United States Of America
c 10 9 8 7 6 5 4 3 2 1
p 10 9 8 7 6 5 4 3 2 1

Contents

Introduction I

Clinical Social Work: Knowledge and Skills presents content to assist students, field instructors, and practitioners to understand the foundation of values, purposes, theories, skills, and principles essential to effective practice. The book offers a biopsychosocial systems approach that is applicable to work with families, individuals, and groups within a continuum of needed services, including interventions with and on behalf of clients. This theoretical approach is in harmony with contemporary definitions of clinical practice.

The Instructor's Manual has been prepared to aid class and field instructors to educate students for effective social work practice. Part 1 provides material on educational theories, curriculum development, and teaching methods. Part 2 presents material related to teaching clinical social work, based on major learning objectives. The objectives are in the same order as the chapters, but also often require use of content from earlier or forthcoming chapters. Part 3 presents suggested assignments for use in evaluating the extent of students' learning. The content needs to be adapted to different levels of education, curriculum structures, and the needs of students in a particular class.

Part One | Educational Theories, Curriculum Development, and Teaching Methods: An Approach to Teaching

An Approach to Teaching |

The multitude of arenas in which social work is practiced and the wide variety of techniques which can be employed render the design and teaching of social work practice a complex affair. Students are likely to be placed in a variety of agencies utilizing a plethora of treatment approaches. Faced with the reality of clients' needs, students are often anxious about exactly what to do. They may request explicit directions from the instructor. The felt need is real. But professional practice requires (1) the understanding of theory of practice and behavior; (2) the ability to abstract and develop principles of practice that are applicable to classes of situations; and (3) the ability to exercise judgment to determine differentially what principles of practice, modalities of intervention, and skills should be employed in each situation. Practice classes are the logical place where this level of cognitive and active learning should occur. The instructor, therefore, needs to create a learning climate through which the student not only masters concepts, theories, and methods, but also integrates the range of curriculum concerns—practice, behavior, policy, research, and values.

Professional learning is a complex process in which the understanding of a concept or theory must be coupled with the ability to do something with that idea. The essence of any profession is action informed by theory and ethics. Practice classes are the place in social work curricula where theory leads toward action. The purpose of a practice class is not to enable students to recite concepts, but to develop their skill to *use* concepts. Therefore, it is particularly important that practice teachers employ models of adult and self-directed learning so that students can test ideas, develop plans of action, and move toward professional levels of skill and autonomy.

A Model of Teaching

The teaching of social work practice needs to be based not only in the content of concepts and theory but also in a theory of learning, especially adult learning.[1] At the present state of the art and science of teaching and learning, there is no universal theory that encompasses all aspects of learning. Each teaching method or approach should be examined with regard to its particular objectives, which often go beyond the basic goal of acquisition of knowledge. The suggested model of learning for use in social work practice is geared toward development of professional judgment and further self-directed learning.

This model connects three theoretical approaches: (1) a basic systems model explaining and grounding the process of learning;[2] (2) a humanistic approach to cognitive learning theory which stresses the individual's capacity of discovery (Bruner); and (3) an instructional and theoretical approach based on a theory of adult learning (Knowles).

Gagne's systems model of learning illustrates the process of learning. It isolates the phases of learning and shows their interrelation. Each phase relates to a process of engagement and moves toward the ability to use knowledge that is gained. While the illustrated phases depict the individual learning processes, they obviously are affected by external events. These external events are the forces which facilitate and motivate or impede the internal learning processes. They include the design of the curriculum, instructional approaches, teaching styles, and methods used in both classes and field work; the nature of the field agency and the clientele which it serves; and the structure and composition of the class, including the characteristics and past experiences of the students.

The systems model is useful for learning professional roles as well as for developing intellectual skills, cognitive strategies, and professional values and attitudes. The use of the model makes it possible for the instructor to design and conduct a course that takes into account the interaction of individual learning processes and the external events that affect what students will learn and how they will learn it.

The humanistically oriented theory presented by Bruner is not in conflict with the systems approach; rather it adds an important element: how learning is acquired and activated by the learner. Bruner emphasizes readiness for learning, the process of discovery, and ability to build linkages between previous knowledge and new experiences to form a unique pattern and process of learning. Freedom of exploration is the sine qua non for development of active and creative control of the learning process. The process of discovery is the means of developing cognitive strategies through which learners control their own behavior. This approach seems particularly related to the learning of social work practice theory and skills because these require conscious and deliberate control of learning and action.

Knowles has formulated a set of principles for adult learning which he terms *andragogy*. The patterns and processes by which adults learn are held to be inextricably related to developmental interests and self-concepts as expressed in active, self-directive learning styles. There are four underlying assumptions for andragogical learning: (1) the adult self-concept of the learner; (2) the importance of experience as a guide to learning interests; (3) the readiness to learn; and (4) orientation to self-directed learning. Adult learning is concerned primarily with issues of role performance; that is, adults' learning interests are shaped by their roles. Professional education can be viewed as a process of role learning, coping with role expectations, and developing competence in professional performance. The integration of knowledge, values, and skills is a prerequisite to competent performance of professional roles.

The andragogical process can be translated in an educational program expressed through the following phases:

1. The establishment of a climate conducive to learning;
2. The creation of an organizational structure for participative planning;
3. The diagnosis of needs for learning;
4. The formulation of directions of learning (objectives);
5. The development of a design of activities;
6. The operation of the activities;
7. The rediagnosis of needs for learning (evaluation).[3]

The social work educator has an excellent opportunity to guide students toward self-directed learning. Most social work students are dealing personally with the developmental issues of early adulthood as well as with the need to develop professional competence. The students' immediate responsibility toward clients in field practice and their desire for professional competence reinforce interest in the subject matter of the courses in social work practice. Content of other courses often seems secondary until students grasp the relevance of knowledge about behavior, social policy, and research to their work with clients.

Social work educators have a responsibility for developing the profession as well as for meeting the needs of students. Rothman offers a useful critique of Knowles's work, noting that the andragogical approach has not dealt sufficiently with the need for mastery of particular knowledge and skills requisite to the development of competent practice.[4] In addition, educators need to differentiate the learning styles of students and to understand the efforts which each student makes toward self-actualization and autonomy.

Students arrive with vastly differing life experience, educational preparation, and knowledge of social work. In addition, they will be at different phases of adult development. Coping with the demands of learning will vary with experience, intellect, and maturity. While Knowles stresses the autonomy of adult learners and the commonalities among them, Rothman argues that, in addition to their drive for independence, adult learners have dependency needs which must be dealt with by the learner and often by the teacher (p. 42). In social work education, the dependency may be heightened by the students' sharp and forceful realization as beginning professionals that people in need are depending on them. This responsibility cannot be assumed lightly and can evoke feelings of failure or a sense of inadequacy between what students feel a client needs and what they feel equipped and competent to provide.

Any individual's progress in learning will move at a rate closely tied to learning patterns and developmental tasks. Dependency needs which surface are not in and of themselves a hindrance to learning. The successful mastery of a task or the ability to learn to work through the particular aspect of dependency alone or with the help of peers or teachers may itself be a vital part of the learning process, particularly in a profession devoted to human growth and development. Recognizing that practice teachers should give prime attention to the individuality of students, Rothman emphasizes teaching as "an art in human relationships" rather than a rigid procedure of instruction.

Acknowledging and fostering autonomy can free students to use the teacher as a resource, rather than as an authority. Teachers need to be able to draw from a repertoire of roles to adapt their participation to the learning needs of students and the course objectives. The teacher's flexibility and ability to respond to the social climate of the group as well as to individual situations can heighten the possibilities for learning. In addition, ability to work effectively in multiple roles may be a cogent device for demonstrating different means and models of learning.

Integrated Practice

A basic assumption of the book which this manual accompanies is that there is a need to teach integrated, generic social work practice. It is essential that students have an accurate understanding of the basic unity of social work values, purposes, functions, knowledge, processes, and skills before preparing for any specialization.

When a social worker has mastered an integrated perspective on practice, the needs of clients rather than the preferences or limitations of practitioners can prevail in the choice of modalities of help. The "law of the instrument" (give a small child a hammer and everything in sight needs to be hammered) far too often holds sway rather than the planned selection of an approach uniquely tailored to fit the needs of an individual, family, or group. Modalities of intervention will often need to be mixed and phased for specific clients. Generic preparation is necessary for careful judgment in combining and sequencing strategies of intervention. The realities of practice indicate that even if one wished to practice only one modality, the demand for such narrow specialization is diminishing. The main point argued here, however, is that social workers need to be able to provide services that are responsive to the diverse and changing needs of families, groups, and individuals.

Students may be somewhat intimidated by a model of integrated direct service practice which encourages learning work with families, individuals, and groups simultaneously through development of generic practice principles. The authors' recent experience in teaching generic practice courses in a master's program indicates, however, that students indeed do learn and value the generic orientation. Students learn to internalize a core of social work theory, skills, and values which they can then apply differentially in the variety of practice situations they face. To be able to internalize the complex content, it is important that students have practical experience in the field with families and groups as well as with individuals. The generic concepts and principles take on a greater sense of reality when they can be tested directly. If students are not given messages that working with groups and families is harder and more risky than working with individuals, they can approach these experiences with positive expectations of learning and success. In fact, if they are given clear messages regarding the advantages of having available multiple means of helping in problem situations, they can move with ease and relative confidence into work with couples, families, and groups.

Practice teachers have the opportunity to orient students to the interrelation of the parts of the entire social work curriculum as a means of establishing educational direction and learning goals. Such orientation early in the first year aids students to gain perspective and control over their own educational process. Teachers frequently are in an advantageous position to assist students to develop an orientation toward learning to become competent professional workers. The practice course in the view of many students, is the most important one. Most practice teachers have faced the earnest student who requests in some fashion, "Please don't bother me with all this theory; just tell me what to do." Such a request presents the opportunity to explore the futility of action and the nonprofessional nature of action which is based solely on techniques and external direction. It opens the possibility for exploring the relationship of theory to principles and skills as a means of revealing the nature and the continuity of professional education and lifelong learning. Teachers are quite likely to be heard if they stress the importance of knowledge from other courses in the development of competence in practice. The practice class then can become the place where both the challenge and the opportunity to integrate the social work curriculum can be found as well as the challenge and the opportunity to integrate practice approaches.

Teaching Methods

Basic Assumptions

Several basic assumptions underlie the approach to education taken in this manual.

"And gladly wolde he lerne, and gladly teche."—Geoffrey Chaucer (1387), Prologue, *Canterbury Tales.*

"There is nothing so practical as a good theory. No practice without research; no research without practice."—Kurt Lewin.[5]

"The whole is more than the sum of its parts; learning and teaching are inextricably interrelated and influenced by the systems of which they are a part."—Mary Louise Somers.[6]

"Teaching is extremely hard work; it is the original and literal brain-drain, being the continual readjustment of one's thought to the thoughts of others, not to placate or even persuade, but to strengthen and enlarge, and make more complex."—Jacques Barzun.[7]

"The ultimate purpose of all education is to empower individuals through a process of lifelong learning."—Malcolm S. Knowles.[8]

A variety of teaching methods is available to the instructor. The selection of methods is guided by the particular objectives of the course which usually encompass changes in attitudes and development of competence as well as acquisition of knowledge about practice and its principles. The particular content that is embedded in the objectives influences the choice of methods. The selected methods should best explicate and illustrate the content and aid in internalization of learning. The choice of methods is also informed and shaped by the instructor's knowledge of the learning process, the structure and environment of the class, external events that have an impact on the process, and the particular learning styles of students and teaching styles of instructors. There are varied creative ways to achieve similar objectives.

Lecture

In lecturing, perhaps the most important element in effective teaching is the organization of content and the clarity of presentation. Lectures in social work practice involve the articulation, exposition, and illustration of concepts, theories, issues, and principles. The instructor's role is to present, exposit, and clarify theories and concepts and to define the relationships which obtain in the translation of theory and knowledge into practice skills. It is an active and dynamic role. The effectiveness of the lecture depends both on the teachers' ability to present material logically and coherently and on their ability to engage students in responsive listening and reflective thinking. McLeish notes:

> As a teaching device it is undoubtedly the most economical method by which the individual can present in a personalized and continuous argu-

ment the general framework for understanding the fundamentals of a particular subject, emphasizing the key concepts and involving the audience in reflective thought that moves in time with the ongoing performance.[9]

Studies of student opinions of the effectiveness of professors in improving their thinking indicate that effective teaching stems from: (1) expert knowledge of the subject; (2) logical organization in the presentation of ideas and materials; and (3) commitment to the subject matter.[10]

Perlman identifies three major purposes of the lecture in teaching practice.

1. *Provision of information.* Lectures can provide information in a tightly organized form. They can set the framework and tone for later discussion or experiential tasks and are particularly useful when introducing new units of study or summarizing major learning points.

2. *Organization and integration of knowledge.* Lectures can be used to organize and integrate knowledge. They can build on students' reading and experience to provide a structure to develop understanding of complex issues, theories, and experiences. They are useful in comparing and contrasting methods and approaches to practice. For example, lectures can creatively structure a contrast of behavioral and psychosocial approaches to practice or can compare and identify the commonalities in different practice modalities. They can be particularly useful at beginning and ending points as a means of grounding and explaining the context for learning and emphasizing major learning and educational issues.

3. *Interpretation and illumination of knowledge.* Lectures can be particularly useful in describing and illuminating the historical context of practice issues. They can be excellent means of clarifying material and interpreting significant differences or similarities in methods and concepts. Presentation of illustrations and exceptions to generalizations, as well as critiques of theories from the instructor's own viewpoint, can aid in clarifying ideas and also in modeling constructive means of analysis and evaluations. Lectures are well suited to both the analysis and the synthesis of material.[11]

Lectures may be either formal or informal. Mini lectures are often used. These are brief, informal, organized presentations which define problems, call attention to issues, or explain a concept. They can serve to introduce material as a focus for discussion and as a useful means of starting each class off on common ground for exploration of the subject matter. They focus and highlight ideas, complexities, and problems and set a tone for analyses of problems which can be carried forward in class discussions or through other teaching methods. They can be used to shape a context for discussion and to conclude discussion and pull ideas together. They are primarily useful as a stimulus for discussion and as a means of emphasizing major learning issues.

It is usually wise to avoid reading a lecture. Generally, an effective method of delivery focuses on major content issues and explanation of problematic points. Careful observation to determine class reactions is a necessary skill for the lecturer. Frequent eye contact with the students enables the instructor to recognize the level of understanding or confusion and to assess the class's cognitive and emotional reactions to the material. The instructor will need to encourage feedback to determine comprehension of issues and reactions. The students' responsibility is to listen attentively to test information for its congruence with their knowledge and experience, and to pose questions when there is need to clarify points or pursue an idea further.

Discussion

Discussion may at first blush seem to be a simple teaching method; however, to be able to direct a discussion and assure clarity of teaching points requires complex cognitive and communication skills. The discussion method, as defined by Potter and Anderson, is "the purposeful, systematic, oral exchange of ideas, facts and opinions by a group of persons who share in the group's leadership."[12] The primary purpose of discussion is interaction in communication of ideas. Discussion, as differentiated from lecture, broadens the stimulus for learning as ideas are presented by a variety of people whose perspectives may sometimes approximate and other times challenge each other's views. Personal interaction is heightened, and feelings and values as well as ideas are transmitted. Participants sharpen their own ideas by exposing them to others. Feedback from the group or from the teacher may aid in refining and clarifying positions, values, and knowledge.

Discussion can be either a stimulating learning experience or aimless rambling. In order to handle class discussion in a manner that is emotionally supportive and intellectually challenging, three types of knowledge are needed: (1) knowledge about and ability to use group process to facilitate exchange of ideas and fruitful discussion; (2) knowledge of learning outcomes which can be achieved through the discussion method; and (3) knowledge about student characteristics which are major intervening variables in helping or hindering discussion and which produce positive or negative outcomes.[13]

Types of discussion. Different types of discussion are likely to provide divergent outcomes. It is important, therefore, to clarify the learning objectives before selecting a particular discussion method.

1. *Mastery of Content.* When mastery of subject matter is the goal, students should read assigned material before the teacher leads the class through discussion of: (1) terms and concepts; (2) the author's viewpoint; (3) major issues and topics; (4) integration of new material with previous learning; (5) application of the material to specific cases or examples; and (6) evaluation of the material.[14] The teacher should take a major role in directing and shaping this type of discussion to assure coverage of major teaching points.

2. *Issue-Oriented Discussion.* Discussion may be geared not only to knowledge development but also to changes in attitude and values.[15] Discussion of issues, especially those in which approaches and values are likely to be diverse, can aid students to clarify their own values and attitudes and help them to become more aware of, and sensitive to, the attitudes and beliefs of others.[16] Such discussion can aid students to (1) develop intellectual skills in analyzing issues; (2) confirm a commitment to pluralism, professional values, and social action; and (3) develop respect for the views of others.[17]

3. Group problem-solving. The third type of discussion is designed to facilitate group problem-solving. This approach is quite applicable in practice classes in which students frequently share common problems, such as how to begin with a client, how to move from an "identified patient" to a family focus in problem identification and problem resolution, or how to assist a group in defining its purpose and goals. The instructor may need to assist students to identify common themes. When these are realized, a class can become an effective problem-solving group and evidence commitment to the solution and direction proposed by the group. Members of the class can also provide a strong support for one another as they take steps to test out practice approaches, evaluate progress and problems, and plan for further intervention.

Skills in group interaction. A general objective of the discussion method can be to help students improve their skills and confidence in group interaction. For professional social workers who will be involved in problem-solving groups, teams, staff groups, and intra-and interagency committees as basic aspects of their work, the discussion skills identified by Gage and Berliner are particularly important:

> working together in groups requires skills that must be learned. . . . The ability to listen to others, to evaluate their arguments, to formulate one's

> own views in the heat of give-and-take, to resist the influence on one's own reasoning of personal likes and dislikes for others, to continue to focus on the problem at hand despite emotional arguments and influences—these skills require practice in discussion.[18]

For students engaged in the learning of professional roles and responsibilities, the opportunity for peer interaction and development of support can be an additional motivation to learn. Feedback from peers can be a major way to clarify what one knows and to spur further integrative learning efforts. Discussion is also extremely useful for the teacher as a barometer of students' cognitive and attitudinal development. Discussion, then, is also an evaluative tool for what is being learned and what knowledge is being used.

The instructor does not abdicate responsibility for the learning process, but assumes roles of organizer, enabler, facilitator, and director of discussion to assure coverage, clarity, and impact of major teaching points. The direction and facilitative control of class discussion are quite comparable to the skills needed in leading task-oriented groups. Attention must be paid to accomplishment of the task of achieving the agreed-upon goals, and also to the process. The instructor needs to be cognizant of the group structure and dynamics that affect the process: group size, composition, cohesiveness, patterns of communication, reciprocal roles, levels and pervasiveness of involvement, and leadership patterns. Each of these dimensions will affect the nature and quality of class discussion, whether discussion is related to subject mastery, attitude change, or problem-solving. Learning in groups is most productive when the group is small enough for all members to participate actively; suitable seating arrangements encourage eye contact and easy hearing; patterns of communication are flexible; and a democratic leadership style is used to promote the free exchange of ideas and shared responsibility for the process and outcome.

In facilitating discussion in social work classes, the instructor has several basic tasks.[19]

INSTRUCTORS' TASKS

1. *Introduce the topic and clarify the goals.*

2. *Ask questions to stimulate discussion and indicate major teaching points.* (Such questions might have been presented at the previous class meeting to assist students in focusing their reading and study.)

3. *Create a climate of mutual support.* Showing respect for students and their ideas sets a tone which makes risk-taking seem safer to the students. A climate of support is particularly important for students who may fear self-exposure or make intellectual blunders in their contribu-

tions. Some students will need support to broach an idea in class, others will need a climate of acceptance to risk expressing a different point of view.

A basic rule, as in practice, is to "start where the students are" in regard to understanding knowledge and attitudes. Humor, if used carefully and gently, can smooth areas of embarrassment. Alternative views can be presented or misinformation corrected without becoming threatening, defensive, or authoritarian. Ways to deal with confused thinking or misinformation include asking for evidence or experience to back up a statement, raising a question about a viewpoint, encouraging further study, and providing alternative viewpoints or correct information. Such redirection of discussion can be handled so that intellectual challenge can accompany a supportive environment.

4. *Structure the discussion.* Discussion may be set up for an entire class or for sub-groups or special task groups. The structure should be related to the learning objective and the type of discussion desired.

5. Maintain a flexible focus. Without sufficient focus, discussion will be aimless, while overcontrol will result in unauthentic communication or mechanical responses. The teacher needs to carry responsibility for integrating ideas and viewpoints and mediating and clarifying differences. If urgent concerns emerge, it is necessary to deal with them and to acknowledge that a different direction is being taken. Periodically, the instructor should take stock of the discussion and point to progress.

6. Summarize the discussion. The instructor recaps major points and indicates further discussion and directions. Solutions arrived at and problems that have been clarified should be noted. Areas of disagreement and variation in approaches should be noted for further consideration.

Completion of discussion should result in increased understanding of issues, mastery of content, or clarification of values and attitudes.

Experiential Methods

Experiential learning actively engages students in performing tasks and participating in interactional experiences and projects. Experiential methods are designed to couple affective learning with cognitive learning as a means of deepening and enriching the educational process. A variety of experiential methods will be presented to indicate the range and possibilities which can be developed to suit particular course issues and teaching/learning styles.

The basic organization of social work education into class and field education is itself an acknowledgment of the power of experiential learning and the need for actual practice to develop professional orientation and skills. As schools of social work accept more students who have little work experience in social welfare, the value of creating experiential learning in the classroom increases in importance. A variety of experiences and exposures is needed to develop a reasonably accurate picture of the nature of client problems and the nature of social work practice.

Perhaps the most obvious use of experiential learning is to bring field experiences into class discussion. Having students prepare process records and case presentations, or discuss ongoing organizational problems or value conflicts of their agencies, adds a convincing note of reality to the study of theory and principles. Judicious use of student case material can enrich class learning and broaden perspectives on types of clients and agency settings.

Many other areas of experiential learning are also available for the practice teacher.

Role-playing. Role-playing, an active simulation of an event or situation, is useful for purposes of analyzing a real life situation in which the class is interested. Role-play can be either formally scripted and prepared or it can be an informal spur of the moment illustration of a particular issue. It provides opportunities for students to learn through listening, directly observing, and taking the roles of clients or practitioners. It provides an opportunity to practice what one might do when faced with real, stressful situations in work with clients and to test out alternative solutions to problems. Students broaden their knowledge and perspectives on practice through identifying with and putting oneself in the place of another.

Attitudinal objectives are major aspects of role-play when students should at least develop empathy for the person they portray or observe. Role-play creates a social environment which may foster creativity in developing new solutions to problems. Role-play can also assist students in developing a sense of confidence and competence with particular types of clients and situations. There is opportunity to try out new behaviors in a relatively safe environment and to practice skills. While the role-play is not a real situation, it is a real social experience for the student.[20] Particularly in social work, where skills in helping depend on both awareness of, and professional use of, self as well as awareness of others' thoughts, concerns, pain, and feelings, the use of role-play can heighten sensitivity, strengthen recognition of the complexity of social situations, and enhance awareness of the realities of one's own response to others and their responses in return. While the cognitive learning from role-play is similar to other techniques for teaching cognitive content and skills, there may be greater retention of learning when cognitive issues are experienced in action-oriented learning environments.[21]

Through role-playing, students often develop empathy for persons initially perceived to be unlike themselves. Much of the research on role-play supports the notion that experiential learning is more effective in changing attitudes than are traditional instruction methods.[22] Attitudes and values are key elements in role-play, and it is important to be sure that these dimensions are covered in discussion of the role situation.

In practice classes, role-playing is frequently used to illustrate practice problems. It is used to illustrate techniques that are suitable for a particular purpose, such as how to structure an interview. It is used to illustrate a process, such as enabling a group to move from initial to core phase. It is also used to illustrate the common and unique application of concepts to types of clients—physically handicapped adults, low-income members of a minority group, battered women. These foci may well be combined. For example, role-play may be developed to illustrate the beginning of a group with abusive parents or a termination interview with a young man with spinal cord injury who is moving from a hospital to an independent living situation.

The instructor needs to provide sufficient information, or derive sufficient information from the class, to set up the situation and the learning goals. Usually it is wise to keep the situation reasonably simple so that central teaching points can be emphasized. The situations should be those that stimulate intellectual challenge.

Introduction of role-play can be initiated early in the term. The students may select partners, interview each other, and introduce the other person to the class. This process can facilitate group development in the initial class meeting and demonstrate basic abilities in interviewing and reporting information and feelings. If the students are divided into dyads or triads which involve the whole class, so that there is no "audience," a ssense of group participation can be developed. When students know each other better, group role-play can be developed in which some students adopt roles and others are observers of particular persons or particular aspects of the situation. To demonstrate varieties of reactions to situations, two different groups might be asked to role-play similar practice situations or participants might be asked to reverse roles to explore the impact of the role on the feelings generated. When students take the role of the worker, it is wise not to have students reenact their own part in a practice situation, since this can become threatening and elicit defensive behavior. When students play clients, there is the opportunity to expand understanding and appreciation of social and individual problems.

Where skill development is the goal and where technical supports are available, videotaping student role-plays and replaying them for discussion and analysis is an excellent teaching tool to illustrate and recapitulate teaching points, practice issues, and principles and skills of practice.

Since role-play often heightens emotional reactions, it is important to debrief students after the action is completed. Usually it is useful first to ask the participants to describe their own feelings and reactions and then open discussion to the class. Post-role-play discussions are a major means of spotlighting and focusing on the learning objectives. Follow-up discussion should focus on the major teaching points and assist students to extract practice principles from the experience. In such ways, the teacher helps the students to connect experiences to theory and principles of practice.

Simulations, games, and "sculpting." Simulations or games frequently are more formal than student- or faculty-initiated role-play. Games have certain rules or parameters which organize and determine behavior. A variety of simulations and games has been developed which illustrate social service issues. They may be extremely useful in helping students to learn what it feels like to be a client and in need of service.

Family or group "sculpting" assists students to develop an understanding of a family or group and the individual members. From a student's case or a prepared record, a student volunteers or is appointed to be a "sculptor." Other students are arranged in a spatial pattern which illustrates the feeling tone, relationship patterns, and perceptions of the family or group members.[23] When the sculptor is satisfied that the "living sculpture" accurately represents his or her view of the family or group, the postures are held briefly for observation. Then members of the sculpture group are asked to describe how the posture and spatial relationships made them feel. Their physical and emotional reactions are compared with the intent and feelings of the sculptor, and other class members are asked to comment on their reactions to the experience.

Satir has made an intriguing film in which she uses sculpturing to elicit the feelings of an emotionally distant upper-middle-class family.[24] The prohibition against talking during the sculpting exercise breaks the normal defensive patterns of the family members while the sculpting is done by a teen-age daughter. The silent experience and the demand to get in touch with their feelings and their bodies aid the family members in acknowledging their own feelings and those of others about their social distance and dysfunctional communication. The use of sculpting exercises, which involve bodily movement, can also help students to become accustomed to movement exercises and to develop awareness of bodily sensations as clues to feeling.

Inquiry projects and presentations. A very different form of experiential learning is the involvement of students in individual or group projects and presentations. Presentations by students, individually or in groups, are frequently used in practice classes. Responsibility for organizing and reporting material to the class is accepted by the student or group. Inquiry models of instruction offer a structure for individual or group presentations and a rigorous process for self-directed and autonomous learning. They are generally based in the philosophical belief that "the promotion of a reflective and inquiring frame of reference will improve the quality of personal and social existence."[25]

The use of inquiry models in professional education requires an andragogical approach to learning and a climate for open discussion and debate. They develop cognitive skills of searching for facts, logical thinking, and developing and testing hypotheses—a process of theory building. Testing and validating facts and experiences and presenting evidence for positions taken become important aspects of learning. The process of theory building concludes with the development of generalizations.

Individually or in groups, students can select projects which focus on their own most important questions about practice. When it is a group project, students need to plan for a schedule of meetings outside class, a division of responsibility for securing and presenting data, analysis of the data, and conclusions to be drawn. The instructor serves as a resource and consultant to the group. The students may be creative in presenting their projects, using role-play or other action-oriented experiences to demonstrate the problem or dilemma and to move through orderly phases of problem-solving.

Inquiry models add rigor to student-initiated projects and aid students in moving from reporting to creating or synthesizing knowledge and developing practice principles. Such models assist students to develop skills in critical analysis and in creative and autonomous learning. If professional education is expected to prepare individuals for lifelong learning, the model provides a useful structure for ongoing intellectual and professional development. If the instructor develops contracts with the student to aid in structuring and developing objectives for a project, the student learns the discipline required to develop any plan for service or program development.

Films and tapes. Films, audiotapes, and videotapes provide a common experience for students, from which they can engage in discussion about particular practice issues. While observing films and tapes is a vicarious experience, they provide a direct stimulus to learning about social work practice. They may be particularly useful in helping students to explore different modalities of practice and types of techniques used with special populations who are at risk. When minority group families and families with handicapping conditions are viewed, for example, students are stimulated to express their own fears and concerns about working in particular situations. Students move rather rapidly into integrating these feelings with knowledge about behavior and concepts of practice. The immediate impact of films and tapes and the shared nature of the viewing experience can help the class to move more quickly to productive problem-solving strategies.

Field trips. Field trips to social agencies or institutions are often a useful experiential learning resource, particularly if they are carefully structured and prepared for. Instructors should consult with the staff who will meet with the students in relation to the purpose of the visit, the specific goals, and the structure and content of the visit. They should provide students with basic information about the nature of the visit and expectations for their participation. When students have an opportunity to learn about models of service or particular forms of treatment, trips can be useful experiences. It is essential, of course, that the students and instructor observe the ethical principles of informed consent and confidentiality with both staff and clients. The opportunities for learning on field trips are varied, but they include exposure to action-oriented creative media, observations of treatment, interviews with practitioners, clients, or members of other professions.

At some point in their education, students should be exposed to the purposes and skills of such activities as arts and crafts, movement therapy, dance, music, and play therapies. The need to help adults and children to express themselves creatively focuses attention on learning the essential elements of these activities which engage the person in creative, playful, and therapeutic processes. Although these can be learned in the class, it is probably most useful to have such approaches and techniques demonstrated by skilled practitioners who use these forms of treatment.

Through one-way mirrors, students may have an opportunity to observe the actual treatment of clients individually or in groups and to analyze and evaluate the processes and techniques that are used by the practitioner. If they can also meet with the practitioner, they can inquire about the rationale for the use of particular approaches and thereby enhance their ability to compare and contrast approaches to assessment and treatment.

Part Two | Teaching Clinical Social Work: Objectives and Methods of Instruction

Essential to effective teaching is the formulation of objectives which provide direction to the learning experience and expectations for successful outcomes. For each major objective, decisions are made concerning the content of the learning-teaching endeavor, the experiences and means through which learning is to occur, and the ways for assessing outcome.[26] Within broad general objectives, more specific ones will need to be formulated to meet the needs of students in a particular course at a particular level of education and within a particular place in the practice sequence.

In this Manual, broad objectives are suggested for each chapter of the book, along with teaching materials and methods that have been used successfully in teaching practice.[27] It is assumed that students will be expected to read each chapter. Instructors find their own effective styles of teaching with each class and creative ways of making the values, knowledge, and skills of clinical social work exciting and relevant to the needs of particular students.

One | Evolution of Clinical Social Work

Objective

Develop an understanding of the evolution and contemporary practice of clinical social work and be able to define and describe it to clients, members of other professions, and the public.

Methods

The first session of a practice class is crucial to the development of an environment conducive to learning and to the enhancement of motivation to fulfill the objectives and engage in a learning process that addresses attitudes, relationships, and skills as well as cognitive knowledge. Learning is facilitated as students become acquainted with and learn to support and help each other to learn.

Unless it is a very large class, the instructor may plan for introducing students to each other. Providing students with a list of the names of members of the class and, if possible, with the field work assignment, will help them to get to know each other. The instructor usually presents the course syllabus, followed by discussion of its meaning to students; explains the place of the course in the curriculum and ways that content from other sequences, including field work, is integrated into practice.

A mini-lecture on the history of practice within the profession that led to the evolution of clinical social work may be helpful. The instructor might distribute copies of the latest definition of clinical social work, eliciting questions and comments from students. These comments and questions can lead to clarification of the terms in the definition or discussion of what the students would like to have changed. It is important that students leave the first session with an overview of the subject and a sense that they know what to expect in the course, and a perception that they have acquired some new knowledge.

In the next session, after the students have read the first chapter, the discussion begun earlier can continue. Depending upon the students' readiness and interests, the discussion may focus on one or more of the following questions:

1. Having studied the definition, what parts of the profession might not fall within the definition and how are these functions related to clinical social work?
2. The vocabulary of the definition is designed to be understood by professional social workers. How would you explain clinical social work to people who are not members of the profession? The class might be divided into subgroups to role-play such situations as
(a) An adult client asks in the first session, noticing the certificate on the wall, "You're a clinical social worker. What does that mean?"
(b) You are in an airport limousine with a friend on your way to a clinical conference. One of the other passengers, overhearing your conversation, asks what kind of conference you are here for. What do you tell him?

(c) You have a field assignment to a pediatric ward of a large hospital. The ward physician is introduced to you and says, "Oh, you're a new intern here. Welcome. I hope you'll be able to calm down the two kids who run around the ward and annoy the nurses." What would you say?

(d) Your father says, "But I don't understand why you want to spend two years just to be a social worker." What is your reply?

3. As you learn about the breadth of clinical social work, what parts interest you the most? With what kind of clients would you prefer to work? In what setting and with what kind of problems? A summary of responses can lead to further clarification of how the generic knowledge and skills would apply to all such situations, but perhaps with the addition of a specialized focus. The instructor can also clarify misperceptions that students can have about practice in some settings.
4. Many students come into social work education with a desire to enter private practice. Instructors might present a lecture on the nature, advantages, and satisfactions and risks of engaging in private practice. They need to clarify that at least two years of practice in a social agency is required prior to entering private practice and the rationale for that requirement.
5. Students often have strong feelings in favor of or in opposition to psychotherapy as a component of clinical social work, often based on myths and stereotypes. The instructor needs to clarify the meaning of individual, family, and group therapy as used in social work practice and distinguish these forms of practice from classical psychoanalysis and other forms of intra-psychically oriented practice.

Two | The Social Context

Objective

Understand the components of the social context and be able to explain their impact on the particular services that are provided to clients in a particular setting, including the effects of social legislation, third party payers, and agency policies on the nature and quality of services proffered and identify the impact of community conditions and populations on clients and their families.

Methods

A primary focus for achieving this objective is on the nature of interacting social systems in a given habitat that support or impede the achievement of clients' desired goals.

1. It is imperative that students understand the agencies to which their clients come and the place of the agencies in the community. It is useful to lecture about the impact of agency and community on services to clients. A profile of two quite different communities and their resources, such as a very poor and a very affluent community, is a good base for engaging students in a discussion of how such differences affect their practice.

2. A frequent assignment is a paper on agency-community interaction in which the students describe the agency in which they are placed, according to the purpose and functions of the agency; its services; its organizational structure; legislation that mandates services and that which places limits on the services given; agency policies that govern the eligibility for and duration of services. Students also describe the community in which the agency is located and/or the one from which their clients come, including its natural and institutional resources, use of space, architecture, culture, and the predominant population groups and their distribution in the community. They are asked to discuss the fit between the agency and the needs of clients.

An alternative plan is to divide the class into sub-groups according to the agencies in which they are placed, possible only if two or more students are in the same agency. This method makes it possible for students to discover and present their findings to the class so that generalizations can be drawn about the impact of the social context of agency and community on clinical practice.

In order for students to achieve success in either of these assignments, the instructor will need to go over the outline of content to be covered and clarify the concepts involved.

3. The make-up of communities and client populations by such factors as race, ethnicity, religion, and social class has important implications for clinical practice. The effects of culture in shaping individual, family, and group behavior should be a current that flows through all teaching of social work practice. Early in their education, students need to begin to acquire the ability to use knowledge concerning human diversity and relationships between and among population groups. An excellent assignment to stimulate students' interest in culture is Spiegel's article on the dominant and variant values of ethnic groups and the use of this knowledge in an ecological model of family therapy.[28]

Three | Theoretical Perspectives

Objective

Acquire a perspective on human behavior in the social environment that integrates knowledge of the biological, psychological, and sociocultural influences on the behavior of individuals in each phase of the life cycle and on the social functioning and development of families and other groups in interaction with the environment.

Methods

The Human Behavior and Social Environment sequence in the curriculum has primary responsibility for teaching the content essential to obtaining the objective. The Social Work Practice sequence is responsible for demonstrating how the knowledge is used in practice. The content of this chapter is complex. It provides an orientation to a framework of concepts that is most pertinent to practicing clinical social work. Students should be responsible for using the knowledge as they progress in their studies. Instructors in practice classes need to fill in gaps in the knowledge learned in HBSE classes. Some instructors will prefer to pay little attention to this chapter at the beginning of the course, using it instead as it relates to understanding the content of other chapters, particularly chapter 8 on assessment when students must have the knowledge in order to make appropriate assessments.

1. The content may be perceived as relevant to practice as students are engaged in a discussion of the areas of content to identify which parts of the knowledge base they have already studied and which seem least familiar to them.

2. A lecture on the ecosystem perspective that illustrates the application of the concepts to an individual, family, and group can help the students to begin to understand the interdependence of the parts and how each kind of knowledge contributes to our assessment of clients. They can explain how changes in knowledge influence practice, for example, the use of drugs in the treatment of mental illness, the renewal of the nature-nurture debate, and the genetic components of many illnesses that have an impact on our assessment and treatment.

3. Several books on HBSE have been published recently that provide much of the essential knowledge base. Students might be asked to identify the major emphases on the texts that they are using in their behavior classes and what they perceive the gaps to be. If instructors are familiar with the books, they can help the students to use that knowledge in their practice.

4. Bring into class descriptions of individuals, families, and groups. Ask the students to identify the knowledge essential to understand developmental tasks at different phases of the life cycle. Include knowledge of cultural factors, health and illness, environmental conditions, and family and group structures and dynamics.

5. Present two or more ecomaps of individuals and families to highlight the differences in the interlocking social systems and their influence on the well-being of clients. Students might also illustrate the complexity of the interlocking network of systems that contribute to their understanding of one of their clients. Carol Meyer presents examples of ecosystems and other graphics in her book, *Assessment in Social Work Practice*.

Four | Values, Ethics, and Malpractice

Objective

Understand the primary value positions of the profession; be able to analyze value and ethical dilemmas in social work practice; develop self-understanding of one's own values and their influence on work with clients; and be able to use the problem-solving framework for resolving ethical dilemmas and preventing malpractice.

Methods

Understanding the full meaning of professional values and ethics accompanies the students grasp of knowledge and efforts to apply knowledge to their own practice. Early in the practice courses, students become concerned about how to integrate personal with professional values and how to judge the behavior of their clients.

1. Give students copies of the *Code of Ethics* and, in the next session, engage the class in discussion of what parts are not clear to them, which statements might create problems for them, and what they would like to see different about them. Use examples as necessary to stimulate students' thinking.

2. Understanding one's own values is essential to understanding those of the profession, identifying conflict in values, and being able to be helpful when one cannot accept the values implied in a social policy; for example, opposition to abortion. One effective teaching method is to

divide the class into small groups, asking each one to select a particular statement in the Code of Ethics, which they think poses problems for social workers and providing incidents from practice to illustrate the dilemma.

3. Select a current issue related to ethical dilemmas, such as reporting child abuse, the "right to die," disclosure by AIDS patients of their condition to lovers, "pro choice" and "pro life" positions, gays in the military establishment, or the rights of birth parents versus the rights of adoptive parents. Engage students in discussing their understanding of those who disagree with them and clarify the emotional as well as cognitive rationale for their own position. When conflict occurs around the positions taken, accept it and use it to teach students about the constructive uses of conflict.

4. In another discussion, encourage students to recall ethical dilemmas they have faced in their work with clients. Understanding may be facilitated by such questions as: What client have you had the most trouble liking? In family practice, do you tend to side with the mother, father, or a particular child? How do you feel when a mother says she just had to beat her child to teach him a lesson?

5. Provide examples of ethical issues for class discussion, for example:

INDIVIDUALS

1) A client seeks a service such as birth control orabortion which (a) goes against the workers' personal ethics; or which (b) the worker personally supports but which is contrary to agency policy (for example, Catholic agencies do not support birth control or abortion).
2) A pregnant fourteen-year-old girl wants to keep and rear the baby.

FAMILIES

1) Parents put considerable pressure on the worker and then on a child who is part of both family and individual counseling sessions to divulge what the child and the worker discuss when they are alone.
2) After four months of conjoint therapy with a married couple, the worker receives a phone call from the husband who states that he is seeking a divorce and is having the worker subpoenaed to testify in a contested divorce proceeding. He states he will have his lawyer contact the worker about testifying, particularly since he wants the worker to testify regarding the wife's acknowledgment of an extramarital affair during the course of marriage counseling.
3) A woman who has been in treatment because of depression following abandonment by her lover after ten years of cohabitation—she demanded that they start a family—moves from depression to rage. In a session, she threatens to kill the lover.

GROUPS

1) A worker leads a group of substance abusers at a county mental health facility. After eight sessions, when trusting relationships have been developed, the worker discovers that one group member has been trying to sell illegal drugs to another group member, who has been having difficulty staying straight.
2) After efforts at scapegoating a nonconforming member, three members confront the leader of the group and state that they want the unconforming member out of the group.
3) In a group for women with problems in relationships with their preschool children, a male social worker becomes attracted to one of the members and invites her to stay to have lunch with him. The member accepts and, at the next session, another member accuses the worker of favoritism.

   In discussion of this example, the instructor can bring up the issue of malpractice. Since students tend to fear being accused of malpractice, presentation and discussion of the use of a problem-solving model in resolving ethical dilemmas and being able to present clearly what they have done, how they have done it, and why, is the best protection against threats of malpractice.

Five | Communication

Objective

Demonstrate knowledge of the concepts of interpersonal and group communication; apply this knowledge to analysis of the process in individual, family, and group situations, and select the appropriate skills for use in reducing problems in communication between social workers and clients, among members of groups, and in interaction with significant others in the community.

Methods

1. The instructor might present a lecture to summarize the essential concepts in the book, pointing out the importance of understanding the major ideas, illustrating the use of the concepts through examples from practice. If these examples are taken from work with clients from varied

ethnic and socioeconomic groups, the students can learn how styles of communication are influenced by different client characteristics.

2. Engage students in role-plays of practice with an individual, family, and therapy group, around a particular problem in the initial phase, followed by analysis of the role-play according to the clarity and problematic aspects of the communication process.

3. It is important that students get the feel of enabling clients to communicate with each other. To help them do this, set up role-plays of families and groups. Students have more difficulty in learning to use the interaction among members than that between a client and a worker. The instructor may, therefore, play the part of practitioner the first time to illustrate the potentials and problems in effective group communication. Or, if the instructor is able to convey the message that it is safe to try out things in the class without fear of being labeled inadequate, some students are usually willing to volunteer to play the role of worker.

4. Bring in vignettes of good and poor practice that illustrate different forms of questions and comments, leading students in the discussion of the effectiveness of the messages sent by the workers and the clients' responses. The clinician's role in assisting clients to clarify their feelings and thoughts should be emphasized.

5. Use brief incidents from video tapes, asking students to listen carefully to what is being said by the worker and clients, asking them to write down the essence of the verbal communication; then read these notes to demonstrate the selective nature of the listening process. Then have the students watch with the sound turned off, and lead a discussion on what paying attention to the nonverbal behavior contributed to understanding the communication process.

Six | The Professional Relationship

Objective

Understand and be able to illustrate issues and concerns in the development of professional relationships with clients and the potential influence of age, race, ethnicity, gender, social class, and sexual orientation on worker-client system relationships; enhance self-awareness of one's own patterns of relating to other people and improve ability to accept, empathize with, and be genuine with a wide variety of clients, colleagues, and significant other persons.

Methods

Students usually enter into professional education with the idea that they like and want to help people, taking a positive relationship for granted. They need to develop awareness of the particular nature of a professional relationship which is based on values and ethical principles, understanding of particular clients' personal characteristics, strengths, problems, and cultural values and traditions. It is easier to say the words than to be able to convey empathy, acceptance, and genuineness to varied clients. Work on understanding, developing, sustaining, and terminating relationships needs to be integrated into the study of practice throughout all practice courses.

1. The instructor might bring into class incidents of practice in which the social worker conveys the characteristics of a helping relationship, asking the students to identify how they identified the presence of the qualities in the process between workers and clients, emphasizing that it is not only the words that are used, but also the tone of voice and the nonverbal messages that are conveyed to the clients. The instructor might bring in examples from work with young children for comparison with developing a helping relationship with a mother who is being investigated on a complaint of child neglect and an elderly man who has a serious hearing problem.

2. Once the students have grasped the essence of empathy, nonpossessive warmth, and genuineness, the instructor can introduce examples of problems in relationship, asking the students to identify the problematic situations and consider how, through imaginative consideration of what it would be like to walk in that person's shoes, attitudes and behaviors toward such persons can be changed. Following examples brought by the instructor, students usually want to engage in discussion or problems they are experiencing in relating to their clients. From exploration of a variety of students' concerns, the most common ones can be selected for analysis of the interrelated practitioner and client interactions that contribute to the difficulty. Typical problems include feelings and attitudes about clients who have abused their children or spouses, engaged in violent or illegal behaviors, clients who are severely mentally retarded or terminally ill, or those who differ from them on some important characteristic such as age, race, religious beliefs, or sexual orientation.

3. Role-playing of typical situations can enhance students' awareness of their feelings toward people who differ from them and ways of learning to bridge these difference through non defensive responses to clients' messages, the use of anticipatory empathy, recognition of stereotyping, efforts to correct distortions in perception, and to focus on strengths as well as problems. They need support from the instructor to know that such reactions are seldom signs of personal dysfunction and that the qualities of effective communication can be learned.

4. The instructor might bring in examples of transference and countertransference reactions to indicate the common ways that these distortions are evident and discuss the ways that workers can handle them through the use of self-reflection and practice skills. To work on these problems effectively, the instructor needs to have established an educational milieu that fosters mutual aid and support among the students just as students need to learn to do that in their practice.

Seven | Intervention

Objective

Understand the categories of skills and the theories on which they are based, and demonstrate ability to select particular skills for use with particular clients in each phase of the helping process.

Methods

Students need to know that there are numerous skills to be used differentially in helping individuals, families, and groups within an ongoing process. Similar skills are employed at different times, depending on the nature and intensity of the worker-client system relationship, the agreed-upon goals, the needs of clients at a given time, the phase of process, and environmental and sociocultural considerations.

1. Given the frequent requests of students to be taught exactly what to do and the danger of the "law of the instrument," the instructor may present a brief lecture on the need to connect the selection and use of skills to what is known about the client system and to the underlying explanatory theory so that students can learn why and under what conditions they use a particular skill. Skill-oriented practice is not sufficient. The

appropriate use of skills needs to continue as a theme throughout the practice courses.

2. A very useful time-honored means for teaching the selective use of skills is the analysis of incidents from process records prepared by students for class discussion of the skills involved, their appropriateness to the situation, the clients' responses to the workers' messages, and the reasons for selecting the particular skills. Alternatively, instructors may bring in such records of practice.

3. Small group inquiry projects have been used effectively in teaching skills. Members of the class divide into groups on the basis of selection of one of the major categories of skills, meeting together to plan a presentation. They explicate the underlying theories, provide examples of the use and misuse of skills, and use whatever media they choose for their presentation, making possible the creative use of such media as play, games, audio or videotapes, role plays, or panel presentations. Group discussion follows.

4. Films or videotapes may be used and critiqued in relation to the skills involved. It is important that students have guidance and be held responsible for the analysis of the material, for it is too easy for the medium to turn into entertainment or a passive experience.

5. Skill in the facilitation of group process, as indicated earlier, is more difficult for many students than is communication in the one-to-one system. It would be particularly useful to bring in videotapes of groups or set up role-plays so that students can observe and analyze the skills used in facilitating interaction among members.

Eight | Assessment

Objective

Recognize assessment as a creative, ongoing, and individualizing process of practice which varies according to the purpose and structure of service and the characteristics of clients; understand the appropriate use of diagnoses of disorders within assessment; and demonstrate ability to make an assessment of an individual and family, using the framework for the content of assessment, appropriate sources of data, and alternative explanations of the interaction between behavior and environment.

Methods

Some instructors may want students to learn the content and process of assessment earlier, but it was placed in chapter 8 because it makes use of the content of all the earlier chapters. A review of the knowledge of human behavior in social environments is essential to successful assessment. Some instructors may want to use chapter 2 in conjunction with chapter 8.

1. Following a mini-lecture that introduces the subject of assessment, students may be asked to select one client from their caseloads and identify the problems toward which treatment is directed. If these are put on a chalk board or flip sheet, they can be classified according to the categories suggested in the text as well as categories of mental or physical disorders. Problems that do not fit these categories might be discussed and grouped into other categories. Discussion of the combination of problems that many clients exhibit can follow, with an emphasis on the need to select a focus for initial work with the client system. Similarly, students might be asked to list and compare the family and group problems
2. If students have not learned to use the *Diagnostic and Statistical Manual* in their behavior classes, it may be desirable to refer them to the *Manual*, make a presentation of the purpose, scheme of classification, and demonstrate the use of the Manual, perhaps with at least two quite different problems. Discussion might follow of what, in addition to the diagnosis, social workers must understand about the individual/family/group environment interaction in order to plan how to help a particular client system.
3. The class might role-play situations in which the worker explains the diagnosis to a client and deals with the client's response to the information given, identifying the principles of practice involved.
4. Engage the students in analysis of first interviews with clients individually and with families to identify the generic concepts and principles used to elicit information for purposes of assessment. Have students identify what they learn from study of the group process that is different from the one-to-one situation.
5. Assign a paper in which students make an assessment of a client and a family or other group, using the outline of the content of assessment in the text. The outline is to be used flexibly to sensitize students to the factors that must be considered in arriving at a psychosocial assessment. Its use, however, will vary with the function of the service, the major goals to be achieved, and the structure and duration of the service. Comparisons might be made of differences in assessment in therapy, crisis intervention, or education situations.

6. Engage students in discussion about the need for generalization and the risk of labeling. Students may be asked to discuss mental health problems with considerable specificity without using labels. Ask the students to give examples, such as erroneous labeling of Mexican-American, Spanish speaking children as being mentally retarded rather than being unable to use English.

7. Present examples of varied rapid screening instruments, such as self-esteem tests or graphics such as genograms, eco-maps, sociograms, and social network maps as a basis for discussion of their contributions to the assessment of individuals and families. The use of an overhead projector is of great assistance in this process.

8. Have students develop role-plays to illustrate different meanings of behavior and experiences related to racial, ethnic, gender, or generational differences. Engage the students in discussion of how they explain the behavior, considering alternative and often multiple combinations of factors.

Nine | Issues in Planning

Objective

Display knowledge of the issues that must be addressed in developing a plan for service; and be able to provide the theoretical rationale for selecting each component of the plan in relation to an agreed-upon purpose with particular clients.

Methods

Planning is usually acknowledged as a major task in social work practice, but it has much less often been carefully studied and implemented. Students need to be taught how to plan appropriate and individualized services with individuals and families and how to form groups to meet particular needs. Planning is a process through which decisions are made on the means to be used to achieve goals. Knowledge of several important decisions to be made is crucial: these include how to choose the appropriate modality of service, i.e. individual, couple, family, group, or segment of community; how to structure the service, i.e., determine its probable duration, the frequency and length of sessions, the governing policies and rules, and the selection of practitioners. This chapter deals with the major issues in planning and chapter 10 with the initial phase which culminates in a contract for service. Planning is a bridge between assessment and the problem-solving that follows.

1. Following a brief lecture that provides an overview of the planning process to supplement the text, ask the students to report on the modalities of practice in their case loads and count the frequency on a chalk board or flip sheet. Then, taking each modality, engage the students in a discussion of the reasons for choosing that one rather than the others. Usually, many reports will be that they were just assigned to work with one person at a time, without being told the rationale for it. This will happen less often with a family or group. When students can give reasons for the selection of modality, list these reasons, summarizing them and comparing the findings with those given in the text. Ask the students to consider whether, if they were beginning again, they would make the same or a different decision about the modality or a combination of modalities and the rationale for these opinions. Discussion of this issue is usually very lively.

2. From their reading and experience, discuss the students' attitudes toward cross-cultural practice in which a worker of a different ethnicity, religion, generation, or sexual orientation works with clients who differ from them in one or more of these respects or when groups are composed of two or more of such populations. What do they perceive to be the advantages and disadvantages of such a plan?

3. Have students bring to class brief descriptions of families and/or formed groups with which they now work or have worked in the past. Ask them to evaluate the suitability of the membership to the achievement of the agreed-upon goals for individuals or the family. From these presentations, draw conclusions about the affect of problems in composition on the outcome of service. The instructor may also bring in examples of groups in which the composition seemed appropriate and those in which it created extra problems for the worker.

4. Open up the issue of the number of practitioners by taking a poll of the students who are the sole practitioners and those who are coleaders. How do they react to the particular role they have? If they had the power to do so, would they make any change? If so, what and why?

5. Set up situations for role-playing with a family and therapy group,

dividing the class into four sub-groups -family with one worker, family with more than one worker, formed group with one worker, and formed group with more than one worker. Give assignments to those not participating in a particular role-play to observe each worker's role and the members' responses. Upon completion of each role-play, ask those who were in the role how they felt about it, followed by the observers' comments on what they observed. Draw conclusions about the values of sole and multiple practitioners.

6. Begin a discussion of duration of service by polling the class for information about the expected length of the services they are providing and the reasons for that decision. Review briefly the research that indicates that short-term treatment of up to twelve weeks is as effective as is longer help, asking the students to comment on these findings. Within the discussion, contribute information about the types of practice that were included in the research and discuss the students' ideas about for what purposes and with what kinds of clients and problems might longer term help be indicated.

7. Have a subgroup plan a service when an individual is the initial applicant and another subgroup when it is a family. The plan might be summarized according to a form that includes the essential elements. Enough space must be left between items for adequate information to be given.

Service Plan |

How did potential clients get access to service?________________

Potential clients (list with ages and roles):____________________

Worker:____________________Agency:____________________

Probable target system:______________________________________

Probable client system:______________________________________

1. Brief statement of impact of context on services:____________
2. Purpose of service and major goals:______________________
3. Brief summary of assessment of needs and problems that will be the focus of initial service:________________________
4. Modalities of service and rationale for selecting a particular modality or combination of two or more: __________________

5. Structure of service:
   (a) Criteria for determining composition of family or group and number of workers:__________________________
   (b) Expected duration of service:__________________________
   (c) Expected frequency and length of sessions:______________
   (d) Physical arrangements:____________________________
   (e) Financial arrangements (fees):_______________________
6. Means of orienting clients to the service and connecting them to the worker who will continue with them or to the group to which they belong.
7. Resources needed:____________________________________
8. Other services which client or members of the family are receiving and how they are being coordinated:______________

The students might choose the kind of service they will plan for or they might be assigned one, for example, an inpatient therapy group for adolescents, a family considering adoption of a child with special needs, a psychoeducational group for parents of preschool children, a young man newly diagnosed as being HIV positive whose family rejects his homosexuality, or a child who is failing academically in the second grade and also having serious behavior problems.

Ten | The Initial Phase

Objective

Understand the major characteristics of the initial phase of the social work process, the major themes, the typical tasks for social workers, the problematic issues that may occur, and the selective use of skills in moving the process toward a successful working agreement; and demonstrate ability to negotiate a contract with individuals, families, and groups.

Methods

It is important that students develop a thorough understanding of the initial phase because a considerable body of research indicates that it is crucial in preventing drop-outs and assuring successful treatment.

Competent intervention requires the skills to initiate, develop, and use relationships constructively, an initial assessment that is appropriate to the purpose of service and the clients' situations, orientation of the clients to the setting and the services, and the formulation jointly with clients of a contract covering the problems to be dealt with, the goals to be achieved, mutual expectations for role behavior and the content and means of treatment.

1. In teaching about the initial phase of practice it is of considerable importance to help students to understand the vulnerability, ambivalence, and fears of potential clients. Beginning students are frequently focused on their own needs and expectations regarding the development of skills and may lose sight of, or overidentify with, applicants for service. The instructor may choose to use role-play situations to help students get in touch with the feelings of potential clients or may have students discuss their own experiences of vulnerability, such as the process of applying for entrance to graduate school or seeking job interviews.

2. Since both students and clients will generally experience high levels of anxiety in the initial phase of work, it is valuable for the instructor to provide anticipatory guidance and experiential learning exercises to help students move toward active involvement and focus on client needs and goals rather than on their own. It is valuable for the classroom experience to provide opportunities to explore and simulate initial involvement with individuals, families, and groups so that students can see how generic concepts apply to different types of clients and service modalities. Presentation of case examples or development of role-plays of interviews with families, groups, and individuals can be used to illustrate the process of intervention and particular entry problems such as client ambivalence, resistance, worker overidentification, or insensitivity to cultural and class variables. Filmed videotapes can also be used to analyze issues when beginning a case. The process of beginning work with groups can be role-played to help students experience the variety of ways that clients exhibit ambivalence and the responses of workers in the early stages of involvement. For students who are often fearful of their ability to facilitate group process, role-playing and analysis of the process are especially useful. Providing students with roles such as children or older adults, which are

quite different from their current developmental stage, can be helpful in moving to an affective experience of client roles and perceptions.

3. Students learn process as they record their practice in a way that summarizes the goals of the interview or group session, the major content, the worker-client system interaction, and as they evaluate the session and their part in it. A format for recording is useful to foster the students' reflective and self-initiating capacities and requires that they apply analytic and evaluative skills to their practice. The recording guide is adapted from one developed by a task force in the social health module in the School of Social Work, Hunter College.[29] The purpose of the guide is to provide direction for learning the substantive content and process of an interview or group session.

Recording Guide |

Worker's Name ________________ Date ______ Session No.____

Client(s) Name(s) ______________________________

1. Objectives of the session:
    (a) What did you have in mind for work with clients in this session?
    (b) Indicate whether and how objectives were affected by input from others.
2. Identification of major themes:
    (a) Briefly summarize the major areas of content—discussion and activities.
    (b) Identify behaviors of clients in relation to content—emotional tone, body language, speech patterns, communication and relationship patterns.
3. Detail two process incidents between you and an individual, family, or group:
    (a) What was the ongoing process into which you intervened?

(b) Exactly what did you say or do?

(c) What was your response intended to achieve?

(d) How did the client or members of a family or other group react? Exactly what did they say and do?

4. Assessment:

(a) Did you and client(s) have the same expectations for the session? If not, discuss differences.

(b) What do you think was accomplished?

(c) What are your next steps in helping the individual, family, or group?

5. What is your evaluation of your performance in this session?

6. What reading was helpful to you in completing this assignment?

The instructor might group the records according to particular types of skills or problems in practice that they illustrate. Through a study of a group of such records, students can develop generalizations about applicable concepts and principles of practice and evaluate the use of particular skills. If field agencies are willing to adopt this format, the class and field instructors will be able to integrate more effectively their particular contributions to learning.

4. Divide the class into small groups. Each group should select (or may be assigned) a particular ethnic group to study. Have the groups plan a presentation to the class, summarizing the literature on the culture of this group and the implications for practice. Based on their knowledge about the cultural backgrounds, values, expectations, and experiences of ethnic groups, the students might present case examples or role-plays that illustrate positive and problematic beginnings with clients of this group. Issues of workers' knowledge and sensitivity to cultural issues should be explored. The danger of stereotyping groups on the basis of limited information should be discussed. Initial work should be illustrated for family, individual, and group modalities of practice.

5. Assign students the task of bringing in reports about a client who dropped out of individual treatment and one who dropped out of a group or refused to attend family sessions. Ask students to describe the major reasons why clients drop out of service. From student reports, compile a

list of the most frequent reasons. Ask the class to discuss the findings. Present a mini lecture on the research on client dropout and note that clients often give quite different reasons for dropping out of treatment than do staff.

6. In class discussion, have students analyze the initial phase of work in the case examples in the text. What are the commonalities and differences in the initial phase in work with individuals, groups, and families?

7. Assign students the task of bringing to class a brief report of the contract they developed with one of their individual clients, family, or group, based on their knowledge of the content of the text. Ask for volunteers to present their contracts and lead a discussion on the generic and specific aspects of contracts with different types of clients and different systems.

Eleven | The Core Phase: Problem-Solving

Objective

Understand the dynamic nature of problem-solving and be able to apply the generic skills of critical thinking, relationship, and intervention, based on a sound assessment, to work with diverse populations and systems of varied sizes and structures with a major focus on interpersonal learning, psychosocial competence, and environmental change; be able to detect and resolve obstacles to effective problem-solving; and understand the theoretical propositions that explain the social worker's part in the process.

Methods

Communication between workers and their clients is built on what has gone before—the mutual assessment of capacities as well as problems, the development of a viable working agreement, the nature and quality of relationships, and the patterns of communication that have been established. The worker's knowledge of human behavior in social environments, social contexts, ethical principles, and communication processes all come into play and are made maximum use of in the core phase.

1. Present a lecture on, and encourage discussion of, the major similarities and differences in social workers' methods and skills of intervention in the initial and core phases of involvement with clients. Ask students to identify how they know and what it feels like when the move takes place into core phase commitment to goal achievement. How does the worker's role and use of self change?

2. Present a lecture on John Dewey's theory of problem-solving and the use that Helen Harris Perlman made of it in her famous book on social casework and its use in group work as reviewed by Mary Louise Somers.[30] Discuss the logic of problem solving, the integral connection between emotion and cognition, and the skills used in resolving obstacles to effective problem-solving.

3. Have the class study the Cohn family record in the text. Ask the students to be prepared to discuss: (a) the problems in relationship and means of coping with problems used by various members of the family; (b) the major techniques used by the worker to evaluate the appropriateness of problem-solving methods of the members; (c) the question, "If you had been the worker, would you have worked with the total family from the beginning of treatment?"; defend your point of view and illustrate who the clients would have been; and (d) the questions, "Would you recommend that Bill be involved in an adolescent group whose purpose would be to enhance capacity to cope more effectively with difficulties at home and at school? Why or why not?"

4. Have students discuss the processes of reflective thinking and the process of helping clients make connections of present and past behaviors and feelings and patterns of behavior. Discuss the dangers and risks of interpretation (premature, inaccurate, or jargon-laden), and labeling with individuals, families, and groups.

5. Provide examples and ask the class to list and discuss various examples of the educational activities of social workers in areas such as child development, parent education, anticipatory guidance for children moving into different developmental stages or into a more challenging social environment such as high school, the experience of divorce for adults and for children, catastrophic illness or accidents, or coping with an aged parent or handicapped child.

Twelve | Multidimensional Services

Objective

Acquire the ability to assess when an individual or family has multidimensional problems which require a combination of carefully selected modalities of practice, professional roles, and community resources; and develop knowledge and skill in adapting generic knowledge and skills of clinical social work to special models of practice, such as crisis intervention, placement or relocation to new living environments, and provision of community supports and resources.

Methods

As an integral part of individual, family, or group treatment, practitioners have the responsibility to engage in services in behalf of clients; that is, to assist clients to resolve the environmental problems which they face or negotiate for clients to secure the needed services. The process of influencing the environment may be carried out through involvement with significant others in the client's social network, with other divisions of one's own agency to assure resources, with other social or medical service institutions to assure access and appropriate delivery of services, and with the courts to assure equal or fair justice.

1. Crisis intervention is a specialized application of the biopsychosocial systems approach to clinical social work practice. Review the criteria for assessing that an individual or family is in a state of crisis, elicit examples from students and from other vignettes of practice. Clarify the special characteristics of this form of treatment in terms of its purpose and typical goals; duration of service and frequency of sessions; major focus of intervention; application of generic categories of skills; and decision-making concerning the use of individual, family, or group modality. Discuss examples of the practitioner's role in cases in which crises occur within an on-going service, such as in therapy groups for AIDS patients or an adult woman who abuses drugs.

2. Facilitating desirable changes in living arrangements through relocation, foster or adoptive placements, or discharge planning is an important purpose of clinical social work in many settings. Such practice requires work with multiple persons in varied roles: individuals needing relocation or placement, their families, significant people in the proposed new environment, and sometimes lawyers, judges, and others in positions

of authority. Present a lecture that clarifies the requirements for successful changes in living arrangements referring to the case of Ed in the text and eliciting other examples from students.

3. Present a mini lecture on the concept of corrective emotional experience, followed by discussion of how new experiences and relationships can have therapeutic outcomes. Encourage students to provide examples from their own lives and their work with clients.

4. Engage students in discussion of their work in face-to-face relationships with clients as compared with work with other people in behalf of clients. Focus on the purpose of the service, the use of relationship, the application of ethical principles to work with persons who are not clients, what skills are used, and typical obstacles to achieving goals.

5. Ask students to bring to class examples of the process through which they engaged a teacher, physician, minister, personnel manager, probation officer, or parent of a child in joint problem-solving to bring about some positive change in the client's behavior or environment. From these examples, demonstrate the application of generic principles of practice to such situations and special matters to be taken into account.

6. In a mini lecture, review the concept of support from chapter 7 and discuss it in relation to support from sources other than the clinical social worker. Ask the students to analyze situations in which relationships are supportive and those in which they may be detrimental in their impact on one or more of the people involved. During the discussion, bring in examples of self-help or support groups that were supportive for some of their members but not for others.

7. Assign a brief paper in which students present issues and problems in collaboration with others in behalf of clients and the nature of relationships and skills that would be essential to resolving these problems. Use examples from their peers as a basis for class discussion and clarification of knowledge about other professions that is essential for effective collaboration and the roles and responsibilities of all parties in the process.

8. In a brief presentation, clarify the distinction between resource consultation and case advocacy. Request that students provide examples from their practice of situations in which resource consultation is desired and those in which advocacy is necessary. Have available some examples to supplement those that students are able to provide.

Thirteen | Termination and Transition

Objective

Be able to assess readiness for termination, understand the complexity of feelings experienced by clients and workers, identify the themes and issues that need to be dealt with to assure a successful ending in different types of practice and different situations, terminate the service with necessary supports and transitions, and engage clients in evaluation of process and outcome.

Methods

The termination phase is often as difficult for students as it is for clients. The process of termination is an integral part of the treatment process. It can aid in solidifying gains, assisting clients in learning to deal positively with separation experiences, and be an important focus in integrating changes in feeling, thinking, and doing. Professional values and knowledge about the meanings of separations at various points of the life cycle and the symbolism of termination should be integrated to help clients and the student to cope with the mixture of positive and negative feelings which usually accompany a termination experience or a transition to another form of social service.

1. Role-plays, followed by discussion of termination with individuals, families, and groups can be used to illustrate commonalities and differences in the worker's activities related to the modality of treatment and to different types of termination, for example, with clients who have successfully completed treatment, with an individual terminating from an on-going group, or with clients who are terminated because the worker leaves, a frequent occurrence when students leave their field placements. They might role play situations in which they prepare an individual or a family for transfer to a new worker or make a referral to another community resource.

2. Presenting a videotape or scripted role-play that illustrates ways to help clients evaluate the treatment experience and the themes and issues in termination can help to bring to the surface for discussion specific problems which students are experiencing with termination. Problems of projection, transference, and countertransference will probably need to be dealt with again and students will need to understand the regression as well as achievement and independence which can take place at points of

termination. A major discussion point with many problems of termination is to have students discuss whose needs are being served by particular behaviors. Helping students maintain a focus on their own role and on what needs to be accomplished in termination provides a structure to help them deal constructively with this complex process.

3. Have students write a brief paper about an experience with termination with a client. What were the client's reactions? What were the student's reactions? What was the outcome of the termination? Discussion of the termination process should include presentation of what happened and relevant materials from the literature.

4. Discuss problems of transference and countertransference which may surface at termination. Discuss the difficulties of dealing with situations in which the client (or perhaps the worker) desires a friendship to develop after the termination of treatment. What is the meaning of this desire and how can it be handled? What ethical issues are involved?

5. Have the students prepare vignettes of practice, using the recording guide to describe their work in (a) preparing clients for termination, (b) dealing with the negative and positive emotions involved, (c) engaging the clients in evaluating their experience in treatment and evaluating the outcome in terms of the agreed-upon goals. From the papers, select those for discussion that best illustrate the major learning needs of the class.

Fourteen | Evaluation

Objective

Be able to select an appropriate plan for evaluating the outcome of the services given within the policies of the agency and requirements of external sources; provide the rationale for the selection of the particular kind of evaluation; consider one's own part in accounting for the outcomes reached; and articulate the components of competence in clinical social work.

Methods

As noted in the text, clients and practitioners engage in a process wherein both influence the outcome. It is therefore essential that the extent to which individuals or families have achieved their goals be determined as must be the worker's competence as it influences the outcome.

1. Present a lecture on the need for evaluating the outcome of services, giving a brief review of the evolution of evaluative research designs, the controversies concerning them, the results obtained, and the ethical and scientific principles that need to be followed in ascertaining clients' movement toward achievement of the agreed-upon goals.

2. Lead a discussion on the policies, procedures, and records used in field work agencies to evaluate the outcome of services. Discuss which ones provide the most efficient and therapeutically-oriented means. What are the advantages and limitations of the use of formal evaluation instruments?

3. Using vignettes of practice, engage the class in analyzing the process by which clients have been helped to evaluate the changes they have made during the period of service, clarifying how the evaluation of results is related to the contract. Ask the students to discuss if there might have been better ways they could have formulated goals with the clients that would have made it easier to evaluate the outcome.

4. Make an assignment for students to bring to class a brief outline of their plans for evaluation of the outcome for an individual client and a family or group. In the discussion of these outlines, search for common and different procedures and skills, including those related to whether the client system was an individual, family, or group.

5. Present a brief summary of the major objectives of the course and the themes that were covered, as a basis for engaging the students in reflective discussion of the gains and gaps in their learning, using the guidelines for evaluation of competence that are in the last chapter. It is important to emphasize that the particular course is only one component of a practice sequence and larger curriculum and that high quality practice will develop only after further study and experience.

Part Three | Assignments and Evaluation

Assignments |

The purpose of assignments is to give direction to students in their learning, provide information for class discussion, consolidate the application of concepts to practice, and integrate class and field work. They are used also for evaluating students' progress and assigning grades.

Instructors need to make decisions concerning the criteria for assigning grades, or if grades are not given, for other forms of evaluation. The important consideration should be what instruments for evaluation provide reliable and valid means of assessing students' performance in terms of the objectives set for the particular course. Students have a right to know, with some specificity, the basis for the grade or other evaluation. That is a difficult task for instructors who often resist the need for differential assessment of students' knowledge and skills. But the instructor has the power, based on legitimate authority, and the responsibility to evaluate each student's learning. Using a variety of means for evaluation tends to increase fairness, providing the instructor has developed clear criteria for making judgments. In addition to some of the briefer assignments that have already been suggested, several major assignments have been found useful.

Assessment

At some point in their learning of practice, students should prepare an assessment of an individual client and of a family or formed group. The assessment should be evaluated according to the proper inclusion of the major components of psychosocial assessment as described in the test or explain why some are appropriately omitted. In this assignment, students reflect their understanding of the knowledge base for clinical social work practice. In preparing students for this assignment, instructors often need to review the outline with the students, assign chapter 2, and conduct discussions of the relevance of the outline to the assessment.

Analysis of Practice

As a major assignment, a paper that describes and analyzes the students' work with clients is a major means of integrating the values, knowledge, and skills of practice. Some time during the practice sequence, students should complete an analysis of their service to an individual client and a family or formed group. In year-long courses, the assignment of an individual may be in the first semester and the family/group in the second semester, because in most field placements, whether appropriate or not, students still tend to begin their field experience with assignment to an individual. These analyses of practice require the students to integrate the concepts and principles of practice into their own work. When the book is used in courses in concentrations in the second year, it can be adapted to those courses, supplemented by specialized reading.

Samples of assignments follow which can be adapted to the needs of students in different courses.

SERVICE TO AN INDIVIDUAL

In preparing this paper, please follow the outline. The recommended length is 12 to 16 pages, typed, double-spaced. As you work on each part of the assignment, cite the reading that has contributed most to your learning, using an accepted style.

1. *The social context.* Provide a brief description of your agency: its services, populations served, and the community.
2. *Psychosocial assessment.* Present an assessment of the client, demonstrating your understanding of the content and sources of information. If a topic in the framework is not applicable, indicate and explain.
3. *The problems.* What is your understanding of the interlocking biological, psychological, sociocultural, and environmental factors that contribute to the client's problems?

4. *Treatment planning.* Based on the psychosocial assessment, present your treatment plan.

5. *Relationship.* Evaluate the extent to which you have been able to develop a therapeutic relationship. What have been the problems in doing so? Give examples of transference and countertransference reactions that occurred and describe how you dealt with them.

6. *Practice examples.* Present two vignettes of process from the beginning phase and two from the problem-solving phase of the helping process. For each of the four examples:

a. Describe briefly the ongoing process into which you intervened.
b. Describe your intervention. Exactly what didyou say and do?
c. Exactly how did the client respond to what you did?
d. What particular skills were you trying to use?
e. Evaluate the extent to which you accomplished what you intended to achieve through your intervention.

7. *Evaluation of plan.* If you were beginning with the client now, would you have the same plan for service or would you make certain changes? Present the rationale for your decision.

8. What value conflicts and ethical dilemmas have you identified? How did you deal with them?

9. If you have terminated with the client, describe the major themes you discussed and evaluate your performance. If you have not, describe your plan for termination.

10. Evaluation of Outcome. To what extent has the client made progress toward achieving the agreed-upon goals? How do you account for the progress or lack of progress?

Attach a Bibliography!

SERVICE TO A FAMILY OR GROUP

In preparing this paper, please follow the outline. The recommended length is 12 to 18 pages, typed, double-spaced. As you work on each part of the assignment, cite the reading that has contributed most to your learning, using an accepted style.

1. *The family or group.* Provide a brief description of the family or group with which you are working, listing the members and relevant demographic data and the major purpose and structure of the service.

2. *The social context.* Provide a brief description of the agency and the community from which the members come. What other services are the members receiving from the agency or in the community? How do agency

policies and community conditions influence the family's or group's functioning?

3. *Major problems.* What are the problems of individual members and group functioning toward which treatment is addressed?

4. *Service plan.* What is your plan for serving this family or group? Did you develop a contract or working agreement with the members? Explain.

5. *Assessment.* Make an assessment of the functioning of the family or group, using the guidelines in the text.

6. *Group interaction.* What were the major problems which developed in the group's membership, relationships, structure, communication, and problem-solving processes that you encountered? In what ways did you attempt to help members and the group as a whole in relation to these problems?

7. *Values and ethics.* Discuss the predominant common and different values of group members and their affect on the group process. What ethical dilemmas did the members' values pose for you? How did you try to resolve them and with what success?

8. *Examples of practice.* Present two vignettes of process from your practice with this group. For each of the incidents:

a. Describe briefly the ongoing process into which you intervened.
b. Describe exactly what you did and said.
c. Exactly how did particular members respond to your intervention?
d. Was there agreement or conflict among the members in their reactions to your message?
e. What particular skills were you trying to use?
f. How do you evaluate your performance?

9. To what extent have individual members or the group as a whole made progress toward the achievement of their goals? How do you account for goal achievement or the lack thereof? Consider the behavior of individuals, the nature of group participation, the appropriateness of the plan for service, and your competence.

10. Summary. What have you learned from work with this group that is different from your work with individuals?

Attach a Bibliography!

CLINICAL PRACTICE IN MENTAL HEALTH

Write a paper on your practice with a client having a mental disorder who is in your caseload. The paper should be 12 to 16 pages long, typed, double-spaced, with proper citations of the literature.

1. Review and summarize the most recent literature concerning your topic. Pay particular attention to:

a. the biological, psychological, sociocultural and demographic factors that contribute to the problem.
b. the modalities of practice and theoretical approaches or models of practice that have been used with clients having this diagnosis.
c. the ways in which the nature of the practice setting influences the kind of services that are available to clients.

2. Using or adapting the framework for assessment in Northen's *Clinical Social Work* and your review of the literature, formulate an assessment of your client. Indicate if and how the diagnosis of mental disorder is related to the wider biopsychosocial assessment.

3. Describe your treatment plan for this client. Will individual treatment, family therapy, or group treatment, or some combination of these, be most appropriate? Explain. Will other resources and services be required in order to reach the goals you have developed with the client? Explain.

4. Present two vignettes of practice, showing what the situation was into which you intervened, exactly what you said and did, the skills you used, and the responses of the individual client or members or a family or group, and your evaluation of the usefulness of your interventions.

5. Critically evaluate your practice with this case. Discuss your interventions which were consistent with your assessment and helpful to the participants and those which were counterproductive. What was or will be your plan for evaluating the extent to which the client or clients have reached the goals that were established earlier.

Attach a Bibliography!

Logs

The assignment of a log, to be used as the major assignment and basis for grading, is popular with some practice teachers because it encourages self-directed learning. In a log, students record their analysis of their reading and practice and their reactions to class sessions. They may be asked to include assignments given by the instructor. They usually submit the logs for the instructor's evaluation several times during a term so they can benefit from the instructor's comments. They are expected to provide examples from their practice to illustrate their use of knowledge. A difficult task for the instructor is to set objective criteria for grading because each student has considerable leeway concerning the content to be included and the style of writing.

The use of logs as a form of note-taking, as contrasted with their use as a major assignment, is an excellent device for encouraging students to take notes in ways that are clearly related to class sessions, readings, and field work. In one place, they will have available to them a wealth of information for use in preparing other assignments, preparation for class discussions, and review for examinations. The log is readily available for reference in solving problems in field work.

Examinations

Although students often object to taking examinations, once they have passed them satisfactorily, they tend to appreciate them. Examinations assure that students will review the reading and class notes and consolidate their understanding of concepts and principles of practice. Along with the assignments that are appropriately individualized, they provide a common base for testing the acquisition of generic content.

Although there are disadvantages in objective examinations, which tend to focus on knowledge rather than critical thinking and integration, they are a means for covering a large sample of knowledge in a minimum time period; they are easy to grade; and can be reliable. They prepare students for today's need to pass objective examinations for purposes of certification and licensing. Many universities and colleges have a special examination period following the end of classes so that a final examination does not take time away from regular sessions of classes. Although quick and easy to grade, objective examinations require that instructors be clear about the specific concepts, principles, attitudes, and skills within each of the major course objectives and that they understand the principles for preparing reliable and valid questions.

Essay-type examinations have the advantage of consisting of questions that require integration of concepts and principles and ability to demonstrate their application to practice situations. If well-designed, they challenge students' problem-solving and integrative competence. Essays are more difficult to grade than are objective examinations.

As a substitute for examinations given in class, take-home ones may be assigned. They make possible more difficult questions and require greater integration of reading with class sessions. They can be excellent learning devices, but it is difficult to be clear about objective criteria to be used in assigning grades when students have access to their books and notes and, unfortunately, there is little assurance that the resulting paper is the student's own work.[31]

Differential grades are very important to students who, too often, interpret the grade as an evaluation of their total selves, as differentiated from evaluation of one piece of their work. Instructors need, therefore, to engage students in a discussion of expectations for learning and the meaning of grades as a means of evaluating a particular piece of their work at a given time. Some students have difficulty in recognizing and claiming their knowledge and skills, tending to devalue themselves while others tend to over-claim what they know and can do. Both tendencies present problems for the instructor in helping students make a realistic assessment of their own learning needs and level of competence. Becoming more able to assess their own competence realistically may be one of the greatest areas of learning for many students. To be able to assess one's own development in terms of professional values, knowledge, and skills is a wonderful achievement. For an instructor to assist in that process is a profound experience.

Notes I

1. Marie Weil, "Practicum in Law and Social Work: An Educational Program in Interprofessional Collaboration," D.S.W. dissertation, City University of New York, 1977; Malcolm Knowles, *The Modern Practice of Adult Education* (New York: Association Press, 1970); Jerome Bruner, *Toward a Theory of Instruction* (New York: Norton, 1968) ; Edgar Schein, *Professional Education: Some New Directions* (New York: McGraw Hill, 1972).

2. Robert M. Gagne, "The Learning Basis of Teaching Methods," in N. L. Gage, ed., *The Psychology of Teaching Methods* (Chicago: University of Chicago Press, 1976).

3. Bruner, *Toward a Theory of Instruction*; Knowles, *The Modern Practice of Adult Education.*

4. Beulah Rothman, "Perspectives on Learning and Teaching in Continuing Education," *Journal of Education for Social Work* (Spring 1973), 9(20):41.

5. Quoted in Alfred J. Morrow, *The Practical Theorist: The Life and Work of Kurt Lewin* (New York: Basic Books, 1969).

6. Mary Louise Somers, "Contributions of Learning and Teaching Theories to Explication of the Role of the Teacher in Social Work Education," *Journal of Education for Social Work* (Fall 1964), 5:61–73.

7. Jacques Barzun, *The American University* (New York: Harper and Row, 1968), p. 55.

8. Malcolm S. Knowles, *Andragogy in Action: Applying Modern Principles in Adult Learning* (San Francisco: Jossey-Bass. 1984), p. xvii.

9. John McLeish, "The Lecture Method," in Gage, ed., *The Psychology of Teaching Methods*, p. 253.

10. Donald Musella and Reuben Rusch, "Student Opinion on College Teaching," *Improving College and University Teaching* (Spring 1968), 16:137–40.

11. Helen Harris Perlman, "The Lecture as a Method in Teaching Casework," *Social Service Review* (March 1951), 25(1):12.

12. David Potter and Martin P. Anderson, *Discussion: A Guide to Effective Practice* (Belmont, Calif.: Wadsworth, 1963), p. 1.

13. Meredith D. Gall and Joyce P. Gall, "The Discussion Means," in Gage, ed., *The Psychology of Teaching Methods*, p. 167.

14. William Fawcett Hill, *Learning thru Discussion* (rev. ed.; Beverly Hills, Calif.: Sage Publications, 1969).

15. N. L. Gage and David C. Berliner, *Educational Psychology* (Chicago: Rand McNally, 1975), p. 472.

16. Gene Stanford and Barbara Dodds Stanford, *Learning Discussion Skills Through Games* (New York: Citation Press, 1969), p. 15.

17. Bruce Joyce and Marsha Weil, *Models of Teaching* (Englewood Cliffs, N.J.: Prentice-Hall, 1972), pp. 48–61.

18. Gage and Berliner, *Educational Psychology*, p. 470.

19. The discussion in the text focuses on material presented by Helen Harris Perlman in "Teaching Casework by the Discussion Method," *Social Service Review* (September 1950), pp. 334–64; Wilbert J. McKeachie, *Teaching Tips: A Guide Book for the Beginning College Teacher* (5th ed.; Ann Arbor, Mich.: George Wahr, 1965), pp. 36–37; Gall and Gall, "The Discussion Method," in Gage, ed., *The Psychology of Teaching Methods*, pp. 166–216.

20. Constance J. Seidner, "Teaching with Simulations and Games," in Gage, ed., *The Psychology of Teaching Methods*, p. 233.

21. Samuel A. Livingston and Clarice Stasz Stoll, *Simulation Games: An Introduction for the Social Studies Teacher* (New York: Free Press, 1972), p. 9.

22. Seidner, "Teaching with Simulations and Games," p. 240.

23. Peggy Papp, "Family Choreography," in Philip J. Guerin, ed., *Family Therapy* (New York: Garden Press, 1970), pp. 465–77.

24. Virginia M. Satir, "Family Therapy" (videotape, black and white, Science and Behavior Books, P.O. Box 11457, Palo Alto, Calif. 94306).

25. Joyce and Weil, *Models of Teaching*, p. 62.

26. A classic reference is Ralph Tyler, *Basic Principles of Curriculum and Instruction* (Chicago: University of Chicago Press, 1949).

27. For classic references on teaching practice, see Bertha Reynolds, *Learning and Teaching in the Practice of Social Work* (New York: Farrar and Rinehart, 1942); Mary Louise Somers, "The Small Group in Learning and Teaching," in *Learning and Teaching in Public Welfare* (Washington, D.C.: U.S. Dept. of Health, Education, and Welfare, 1963), pp. 158–73; reprinted in Council on Social Work Education, *Source Book of Readings on Teaching in Social Work* (New York: CSWE, 1963), pp. 1–18; Charlotte Towle, *The Learner in Education for the Professions* (Chicago: University of Chicago Press, 1954).

28. John P. Spiegel, "An Ecological Model with an Emphasis on Ethnic Families," in Eleanor Reardon Tolson and William J. Reid, eds., *Models of Family Treatment* (New York: Columbia University Press, 1981), pp. 121–58.

29. Elaine Marshack, "Student Recording in Social Health Agencies," in Phyllis Coroff and Mildred Mailick, eds., *Social Work in Health Settings* (New York: Prodist, 1980), ch. 7.

30. Helen Harris Perlman, *Social Casework: A Problem-Solving Process* (Chicago: University of Chicago Press, 1957); Mary Louise Somers, "Problem-Solving in Small Groups," in Robert W. Roberts and Helen Northen, eds., *Theories of Social Work with Groups* (New York: Columbia University Press, 1976).

31. Edward J. Saunders, "Confronting Academic Dishonesty," *Journal of Social Work Education* (Spring/Summer, 1993), 29(2):224–31.